GLADYS CONKLIN

Praying Mantis

The Garden Dinosaur

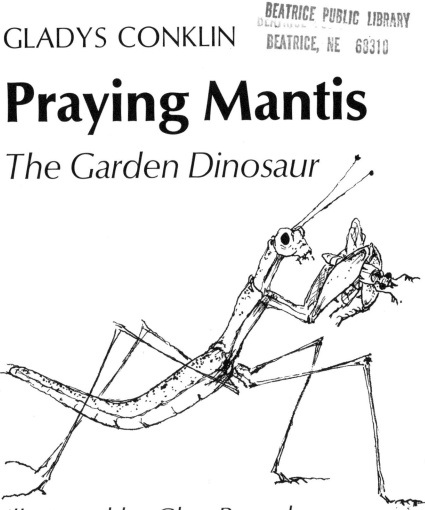

illustrated by Glen Rounds

HOLIDAY HOUSE · NEW YORK

*To all my friends
who kept asking me
throughout the past year,
"What subject are you working on now?"
Here it is!*

Library of Congress Cataloging in Publication Data

Conklin, Gladys Plemon.
  Praying mantis, the garden dinosaur.

  1. Praying mantis—Juvenile literature.
I. Rounds, Glen, 1906- II. Title.
QL508.M2C66   595.7'25   77-27007
ISBN 0-8234-0323-8

Author's note

Over one thousand species of mantises are found in the tropics but very few in North America. The two familiar ones found on both coasts are the *Stagmomantis carolina* and *Tenodera sinensis*. The two-inch-long Carolina mantis is a native, and the four-inch Tenodera came from China as a stowaway on a ship. The Tenodera is the one described in this book.

As a house pet, the mantis immediately becomes the center of attention. When company enters the room, she turns her head and looks over her shoulder as a person does. No other insect can do this. This action makes you feel that she really responds to you.

She'll hold out her front legs as though asking to be picked up. She is so appealing that you tend to forget that she is the dreadful ogre to all smaller insects that come near her. She is a cannibal—she eats other mantises, even her mate.

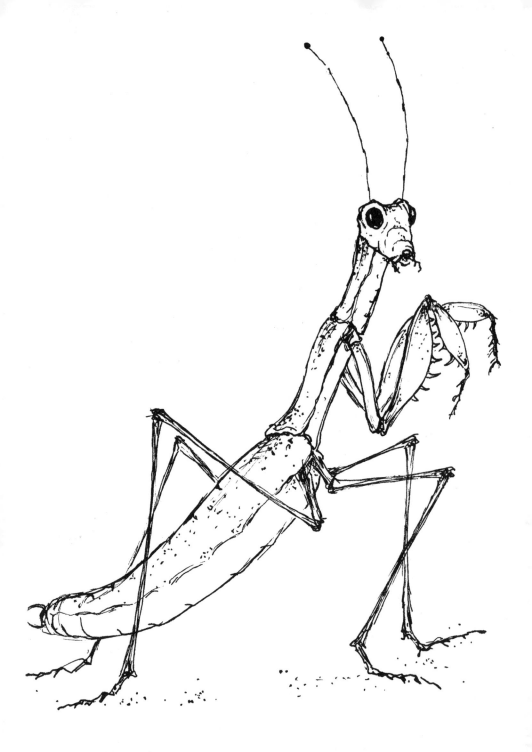

The praying mantis is my favorite
insect. It's fun to watch one grow up.
My mother bought a praying mantis
egg case at the plant nursery.
I tied it on a bush in our backyard.

I looked at the egg case every morning.
On the case was a narrow
strip of thin plates that over-
lapped like shingles on a roof.
The edges of these plates were loose
and that was where the young mantises
would slip out.

One morning the egg case was swarming
with tiny praying mantises. They
dangled head down from soft white
threads attached to the egg case.
Each mantis was closely wrapped in a
clear sac. I could see them twisting
and turning inside the sacs.

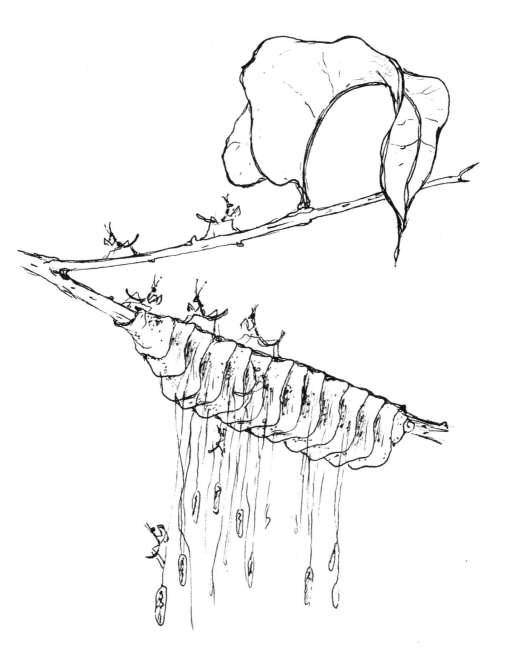

While I watched them, some of the sacs
broke open and the little mantises
were free. Their feet reached up and
they quickly climbed over the swinging
mass of mantises above them.

Most of the little mantises hurried
under the leaves and out of sight.
One stood still and looked at me.
She wasn't much bigger than a mosquito.
She had a pointed face and
two large dark eyes.

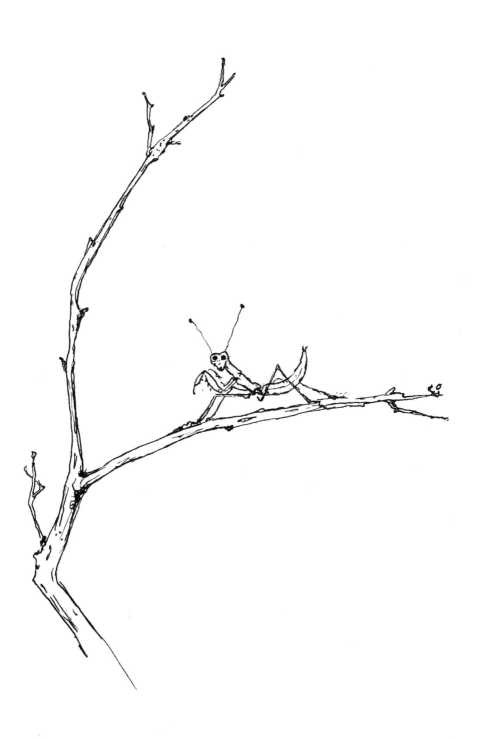

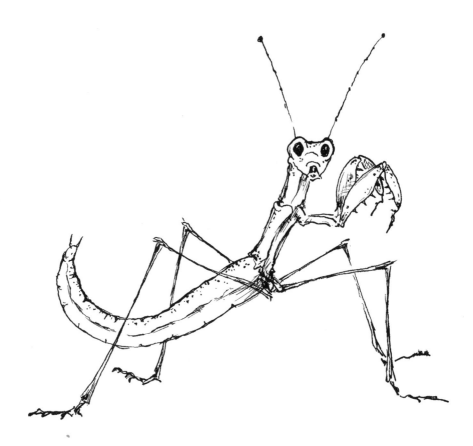

Her front legs were covered with sharp
spines. She carried them high and folded,
as if she were praying. That's why she's
called a praying mantis. She wasn't
praying. The spines were a trap
for catching live food.

I looked again in the afternoon
and was just in time to see
a mantis catch an aphid.
His spiny front legs shot out
and snapped together around the insect.

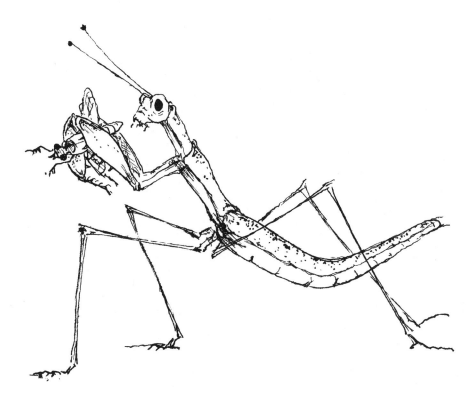

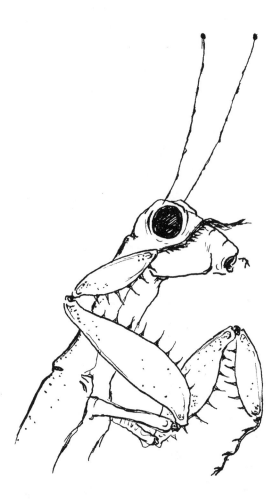

I watched him eat the aphid.
When he finished, he washed his face.
He used his front feet and carefully
cleaned from side to side
just the way my cat does.

Gently and slowly he wiped each
large eye. He pulled each of his legs
through his mouth. He nibbled
and wiped between all the spines.

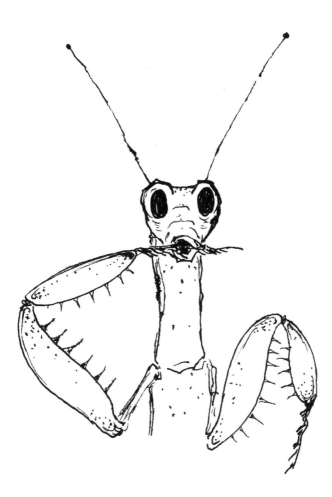

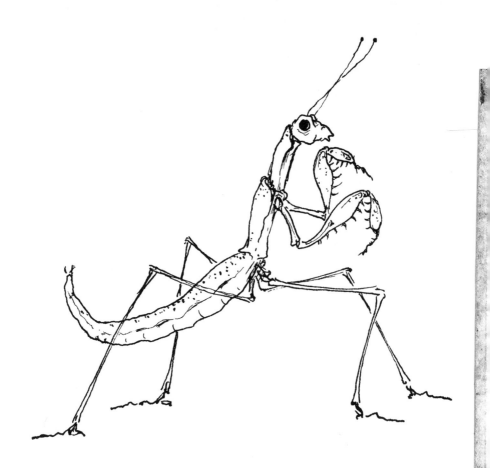

A praying mantis seems to spend
most of its life eating. I tried
to keep one in my room, but I couldn't
find enough small insects for it.
I put it on a bush outside
to catch its own food.

When the little praying mantises
can catch larger insects, they'll find
our yard full of good food.
Every day I see beetles and butterflies
and crickets, and katydids and
grasshoppers and caterpillars.

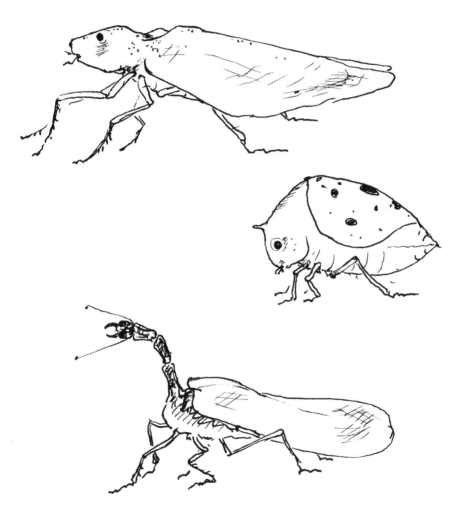

One day I saw a praying mantis
hanging upside down from the edge of
a leaf. She was getting ready to shed
her old skin and get a larger one.
Her skin was really her skeleton,
but mantis skeletons don't grow.

I watched her tight skin split open
down her back. Her body pulled and
tugged and slipped out of the old skin.
Slowly her long legs pulled free.
Then her new antennas and pointed face
followed, and she was shiny new.

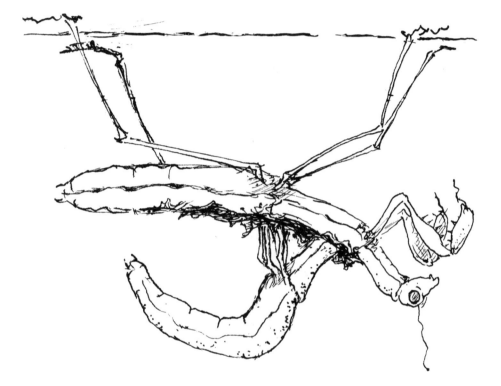

She hung there quietly for a
few minutes. She was waiting for her
new skin to dry. Soon she moved away
and left her white skeleton
hanging from the leaf.

A mantis has to shed its skin
five or six times as it grows.
The last time it slips out
of its skin, it will have a
pair of beautiful wings.

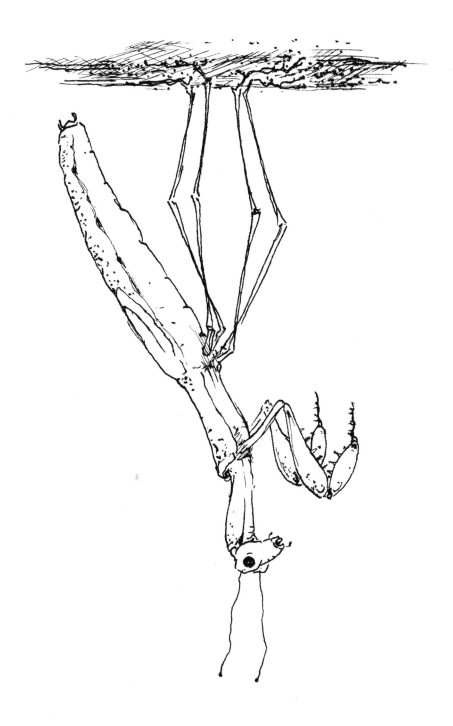

I know the difference between a male
and a female praying mantis.
When a female has her wings, she has
a fat round belly full of eggs.
The male is slender, and smaller
than the female.

I watched two of them one day.
The male stood still and stared
at the female. Slowly he moved
closer and closer. Suddenly he rushed
and jumped upon her back.
He stayed with her for many hours.

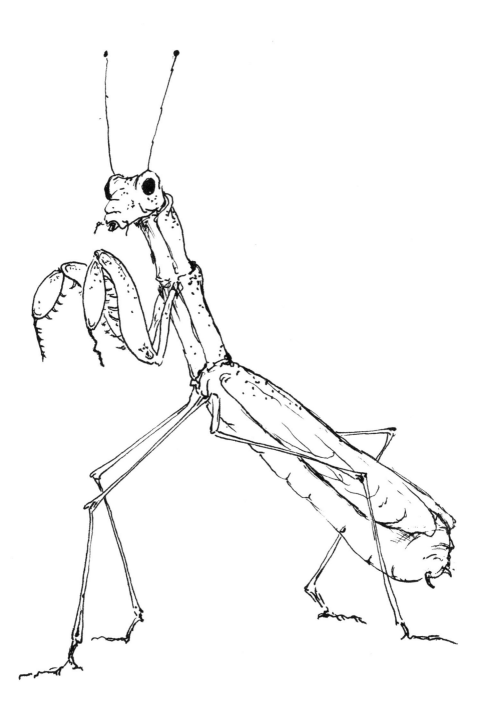

When they separate, the male has to move
quickly. If the female is hungry, she may
grab him and take a bite out of his neck.
He never tries to get away. Bite by bite
she finishes him. She eats all but his
dry wings and legs. After cleaning
her face, she moves on to look for
a cricket or a katydid.

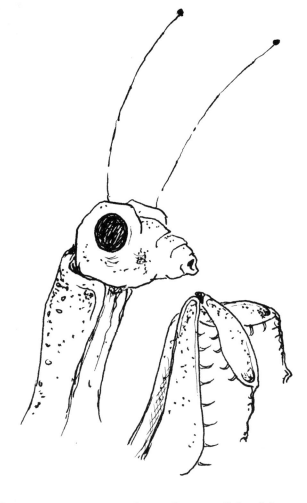

She soon stopped and stood half-erect
in a praying position. Only her eyes
moved as she watched for food.
A grasshopper leaped up on the leaf
in front of her. There was a quick flash
of her spiny front legs, and the
struggling grasshopper was caught.

One day I found a female praying mantis
hanging upside down on a stem. A lot of
thick foamy bubbles were coming
out of her body. Her back end
was moving in small circles in the foam.

She was laying her eggs, and the bubbly
foam was to cover and protect them
after it dried. For one whole hour
she worked until the last egg was laid
and the sturdy egg case was finished.

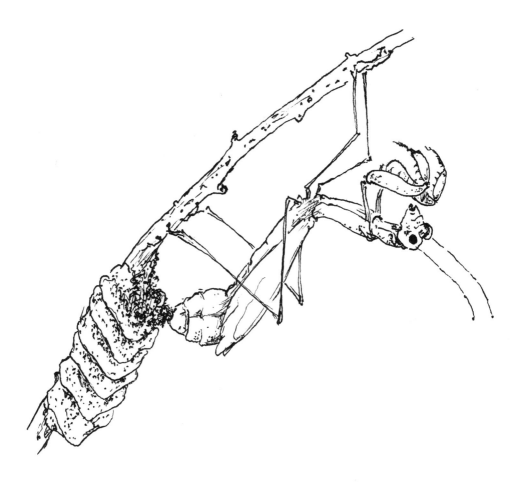

An egg case is about the size of
a large walnut. It has to be strong,
because it will be outdoors all winter.
Rain and hail will pound against it.
High winds will blow on it, and
snow will cover it for a long time.

When you cut open an empty egg case,
you can see that the eggs are
in straight rows in the middle.
There may be a hundred or even as many
as three hundred eggs in one case.

I watched her all the time
she was working.
She didn't turn around once
to look at what she was making.

She didn't need to look at what
she was making. There were organs
inside her body that did the
work for her. When the last egg was
covered up, the praying mantis
climbed down the stem and walked away.
That was the last I saw of her.

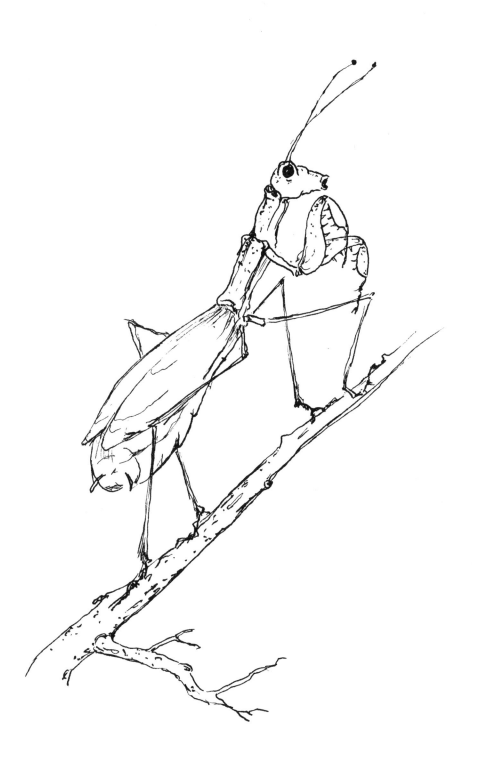

A pet praying mantis

An adult female mantis makes an interesting pet. It's important to have a female, not a male. The male mantis never seems to be "friendly" with people. He won't sit on your finger and gaze at your friends. He won't hold out his front legs as though asking to be picked up.

The female mantis "makes friends" quickly and is most amusing. If you can get permission from your parents, put your mantis on a kitchen curtain (where I keep mine) or on your bedroom curtains. She'll probably stay there because the female seldom if ever flies.

You'll have to hand-feed her either live insects or small bits of raw liver on a toothpick. Move the toothpick back and forth close to her face, and she'll learn to take it. She'll grab the toothpick and hold it as you might hold an ear of corn. If you live in the city, you can usually buy crickets at pet shops.

Be sure to give her water every day. She won't

drink out of a dish, but hold a teaspoonful of water to her mouth and she will soon take it.

You may find a terrarium or a small fish tank a good thing in which to keep your mantis. She will need a few twigs or sticks in the terrarium to climb on, and also a firm stem on which to make her egg case.

No matter how well you feed her, she will soon die because her life comes to a natural end in the late fall. In the southern states the mantises live longer.

G.C.